HOW TO PUTT LIKE A PRO

IN 4 SIMPLE STEPS

Frank Muir

Published by JHJ22 Publishing

ISBN 978-0-9932518-3-2

AUTHOR NOTE

This self-help booklet is an updated and reworked version of my earlier self-help booklet – HOW TO CURE YOUR PUTTING YIPS IN 4 SIMPLE STEPS. If you have purchased, or have already read that booklet, then please note that the same techniques for improving your putting are detailed here. If you have not come across my earlier booklet, then I encourage you to read on to discover 4 simple steps that will change your putting forever, and have you holing putts like a pro – in no time at all.

If you're asking why I would bother to update and rework my already successful booklet – HOW TO CURE YOUR PUTTING YIPS IN 4 SIMPLE STEPS – here is the answer.

Through many informative and drink-stimulated chats at the 19th hole I came to realise that many middle-handicap golfers – in fact, almost everyone I spoke to – had the same poor putting techniques as those unfortunate souls who suffer from the dreaded putting yips, without knowing it. I would mention my self-help booklet to them as a possible cure, but no one was interested in curing something they believed they didn't have – why would they? Any advice I tried to impart invariably fell on deaf, and mostly stubborn, ears.

I found this puzzling, until I came to understand that their dismissal of the phrase 'putting yips' was in fact a form of denial, a bit like an alcoholic continuing to drink, trying to convince himself and others around him that he has no problem. That was the moment of epiphany for me, when I suddenly understood that most golfers did not associate their own poor putting techniques with those of the yips, and that in order to help them, I needed to retitle and rework my self-help booklet.

So, if you struggle with your putting – ***no matter what the cause*** – then this booklet is for you. If you want to become a better putter, gain confidence on the greens, or shave a few strokes or more off your card, then I invite you to read on and learn how to **PUTT LIKE A PRO IN 4 SIMPLE STEPS**.

CHAPTER 1

INTRODUCTION

If you're reading this self-help booklet it's because like many amateur golfers, you are not a great putter. You may have already assigned that negative belief to your subconscious as an irrevocable fact of your golfing life – You are a bad putter. End of. Or maybe you are suffering, or have suffered, from that most debilitating of all golfing inflictions – the putting yips. Well, you don't have to worry any more – not because millions of golfers around the world are poor putters like you, or have been struck down with the yips, so you are not alone in your misery – but because what you are about to read will not only cure all your putting troubles – ***whatever they are, yips or not*** – but will assign them to the golfing dump forever.

And you won't have to spend a fortune booking a session of lessons with your golf pro, or worse, a sports psychologist. For nothing more than the cost of a cup of coffee – depending on where you live, and what coffee you drink, of course – you have purchased this self-help booklet that will show you how to improve your putting and fix all your putting flaws – ***forever*** – and have you holing more putts than you ever dreamed possible.

If you struggle with your putting, I have no doubt that you'll have tinkered around to find a cure. You'll have tried different putting techniques, tried all sorts of different putters, and fiddled about with a dozen or so other things, looking for a cure. Of course you have. You want to improve your putting. We all do. After all, putting should be the easiest part of the game. But if I were a betting man, I would bet that none of these 'cures' worked – at least not in the long-term.

And if you suffer from the putting yips, I'm sure you've heard that once you have them, you have them for life. So you've probably just given in to the idea that your putting is as good as it's ever going to get. There is no cure, so what's the point of even trying?

Well, you haven't got the yips for life. Believe me. And to all struggling putters – ***yips or not*** – by following my simple 4-step process, your putting will improve – ***no matter what the cause***. Poor putting and soul-destroying putting yips will become a thing of the past, a distant memory, because you are about to tackle your putting troubles at the very heart of the problem – ***you***.

CHAPTER 2

WHO AM I?

Well, first of all let me tell you who I am not. I am not a professional golfer, nor am I some marketing guru intent on screwing you out of your money. I am just a regular guy who once suffered from the putting yips, but who found a cure through trial and error, and who only wants to share his 'secret' with as many 'broken' golfers as possible. In fact, although I am a member of my local golf club, I have not hit a golf ball for almost two years (as of the writing of this booklet) due to an injury on my shoulder. At the end of this booklet you will find my website address, and you can learn a bit more about me and what I now do for a living. Feel free to contact me if you want, hopefully to tell me that your putting troubles are a thing of the past.

Why do I believe that I can help you where others – presumably – have failed? Well, let me tell you a story. Years ago, when I was in my early twenties, I was a fairly decent golfer with a handicap of 2, at a time when the best golfer in the British Isles played off +2 (the handicapping system back in the 70s was more demanding than it is now – ask anyone who knows anything about golf). I represented Dunbartonshire County on three separate occasions, at a time when the regular team consisted mostly of internationalists, one or two of whom were arguably the best golfers in Britain, having played in the Walker Cup. That record doesn't sound like much, but I was proud of that achievement. I was also proud of equalling the (then) course record at my local golf club when I shot a 3-under par 66 with a ball out of bounds at the sixteenth.

So, I was a pretty good golfer in my day, with a decent game of golf, and a lot of potential. But I could have been better. I could have been much, much better. I know I could have. If I had stuck at it I could have cut my handicap to 1, then to scratch, maybe even played for my country, Scotland – an early goal of mine. I could have taken my game more seriously. I could have practised more instead of spending too much time trying to birdie that damned 19th hole – from time to time I even eagled it! I could have taken professional lessons. I could have had a golfing mentor. I could have, I could have, I could have…

Instead, what happened was that I developed the putting yips, and rather than lowering my scores, my handicap, and improving my game, I found my game had bottomed out, with next to no chance of ever improving. I was beaten. And I knew it. I was a bit of a hot-headed youngster back then, and with every rising score and missed putt, my anger, frustration, and self-pity mounted. The harder I tried, the more my yips gripped me, and in a surprisingly short space of time – a few months as best I recall – I threw in the towel, sold my golf clubs, and went on my way, my golf game more or less destroyed by the putting yips.

I would be lying if I said I never tried to play again. Over the years, the golfing bug would get to me, and I'd play a round of golf using a set of borrowed clubs. But time had healed nothing. My putting yips were still there, my confidence on the greens was shot, and my ability to play golf to a fairly decent level no more than a distant, fading memory.

Then one day I decided to take up the game again, this time for nothing more than pleasure and a bit of exercise chasing a wee white ball. The yips wouldn't matter to me anymore. It wouldn't matter if I couldn't break 80, maybe even 90. Golf for me would become a day's exercise, a walk in the fresh air, a chance to take things easy. Or so I thought! I bought myself another set of clubs, and set about it, but soon found that having once been a fairly decent golfer, settling for anything less just wasn't going to cut it.

So I made a decision. I was going to cure the putting yips, or die trying. The fact that I am alive and writing this self-help booklet – passing on the wisdom, if you like – proves that I did indeed cure my putting yips.

And I can cure your poor putting, too.

Read on, and you will discover the jaw-droppingly simple techniques I used to overcome my putting yips – ***forever*** – and how you, too, can assign your own putting troubles to the golf dump for the remainder of your soon-to-be-happy golfing life.

CHAPTER 3

WHAT ARE THE YIPS?

Whether or not you believe you don't suffer from the putting yips *per se*, you should read this chapter, because the yips take many insidious and innocuous forms. If you're a poor putter, you more than likely have some form of the yips without realising you have them. So, from this point on, throughout this booklet when I refer to 'putting yips' I am referring to any poor putting techniques or actions that cause you to miss putts when you know you should be holing them.

Well, what exactly are the yips? There are as many different answers to that question as there are holes in a dozen golf courses, and probably as many different cures as there are yards in these courses, maybe even feet! You get the gist of what I'm saying, I'm sure.

Simply put, the putting yips can refer to any number of twitches, jerks, pauses, hand movements, forward presses, or any other motor control abnormalities that seem to spring up before or during an attempt to commit to a putting stroke. The putting yips are most dominant when the golfer is faced with a putt he knows he can make, but fears missing – you got it in one – that dreaded three-footer. The resulting loss of confidence on the greens will almost certainly over time spread into every aspect of the golfer's game, removing any vestige of pleasure from playing a round of golf, and turning it into an insurmountable miserable challenge, rather than a game to be enjoyed and improved upon.

The term *yips* is believed to have been coined by the late, great Tommy Armour who once proclaimed, "Once you've had 'em, you've got 'em," meaning, there is no cure. Well, with all due respect to Mr Armour, if you don't mind my saying so, he was wrong. He was oh, so wrong, because I cured my putting yips, and I know I can cure yours, too.

Let me start by explaining how my putting yips affected me. Dead easy. I froze. Plain and simple. I would carefully figure out the break, line up the putter head, know exactly where and how hard I was going to strike the ball, then… then…?

That was it. I was stuck. I couldn't take the putter back. I'd walk away, then try again, but the result was always the same. In the end, I found out that the only way I could begin the putting stroke was to take a forward press with my hands first, which drove me to frustrated distraction. I tried to live with it for a while, but the longer it went on, the more prominent my forward press became, until I realised that all the care I'd taken in aligning my putts was being destroyed by that forward press. When I stroked the ball, more often than not I would send it off on a slightly different line from the one I'd chosen. The end result was that my putting was a lottery. I missed more putts than I holed, and the sight of a three-foot putt would have me gritting my teeth and my hands literally shaking from the thought of missing it. Oh, I could still drive the ball as well and as far as the best golfers. I could still drill a long iron onto some faraway green with a ball flight and power that had higher handicappers looking on with envy and awe. But when it came to trying to putt that ball into the hole, I was no better than a 24-handicapper.

But I overcame my putting yips. And now, so can you.

CHAPTER 4

THE CAUSE OF POOR PUTTING

You may, or may not, be surprised to learn that the cause of the putting yips, or just plain poor putting, is not a mechanical issue. Your technique may break down during the putt, of course, but that is not the root cause of the problem. So trying to fiddle with your technique, or changing your grip, or your putter, is not the answer. It's like whacking a weed. It looks like you've got rid of the damn thing, but you won't until you get to its root and tear it out. And that's what this booklet is going to do for your putting. Get to the root of the problem – ***you*** – and sort you out, once and for all.

On one hand, you may not like to hear that the real cause of your poor putting is ***you***. But over time your own mind has become conditioned to respond in a particular way when you prepare to commit to a putt. On the other hand, that makes your poor putting easy to cure. Trust me on that, because the way out of the problem lies inside ***you***. You must strengthen and condition your mind to remain calm and focused when you're about to putt.

Now before you groan and moan in despair, and say that this self-help booklet was nothing more than a hoax, that you just knew your putting was going to be fixed by sitting cross-legged on a rug with your eyes closed and chanting mind-relaxing mantras through joss-stick smoke, just relax, will you? That's not the answer. Nowhere close.

So bear with me, and read on.

CHAPTER 5

GETTING RID OF YOUR PUTTING FLAWS

Putts between 4 and 6 feet are ones that we expect to make most of the time, but research apparently confirms that even professional golfers on average make about 50 per cent of their 6-foot putts. So the average golfer should not get too frustrated when their percentage is lower. However, by way of this booklet I will show you 4 simple steps that will train your mind to slot putt after putt after putt without the slightest signs of any putting flaws.

So, what is this magical cure? Apparently, some serious research into putting established that golfers with the yips have rapid eye movements during the stroke, which interferes with the brain-to-muscle control. The cure to the yips in these cases is simple – all you have to do is focus on the hole, then close your eyes and putt. Simple, isn't it? Well, you wouldn't drive your car down the main street with your eyes closed, so why in the world would you hit a golf ball with your eyes closed? In other words, this is just one of the multitude snake-oil cures that float around the planet. The game of golf is full of them, and I doubt if any of them will fix the root cause of your putting yips with any permanence.

So let's get started.

The first thing you must do to rid your game of your putting flaws is to take responsibility for them. Poor putting, and the putting yips *per se*, is not a mechanical flaw. The flaw is in you. Let me repeat that. *The flaw is in **you***. Plain and simple. Once you understand that, and take ownership of your putting, you can stop looking for mechanical cures, stop buying all sorts of putters, stop fiddling with all sorts of putting grips, and start to look for answers inside yourself. *The flaw is in **you***. This is where the problem lies. With ***you***. You have to take that on board, and understand it. *The flaw is in **you***. Nowhere else.

Also understand that the mind is a powerful instrument. We all know its effects on our golf swing. Negative pre-shot thoughts like 'don't put it in the water' more often than not result in a poor shot followed by lifting and dropping from the water under penalty. So, if you force your thoughts to concentrate on hitting the fairway or the green, and you trusted your swing, would the brain make it happen? Similarly, if you focused your thoughts on putting the ball into the hole, and you trusted your stroke, would it work?

The simple answer is – yes.

Your goal, and the answer to curing your putting yips forever, is to remove all negative thinking from the putt and allow your reflexes and muscle memory to take over on automatic and get the job done. I want you to read that sentence again, and again, and again, and one more time for good luck. In fact, I want you to read that sentence as many times as necessary until you fully and totally understand what it means. *Your goal is to remove all negative thinking from the putt and* ***allow your reflexes and muscle memory to take over on automatic*** *and get the job done.* This booklet will show you how to do just that, without spending one more cent, without leaving the comfort of your home, without wasting endless hours on the golf course, and without breaking any golf clubs or tearing your hair out in despair.

Solid fundamentals are the key to improving your putting. Understand that your brain is causing you to miss putts simply because your body does not feel comfortable with the shot you're about to make. So, let's start by making you feel comfortable, by focusing on that most fundamental of fundamentals – your putting stroke.

CHAPTER 6

STEP 1

DEVELOP A SOUND PUTTING STROKE

If you're like me and you watch a lot of tournament golf on TV, you've more than likely seen a bunch of different putting styles – claw grips, cack-handed grips, reverse claw grips, belly putters, and a dozen or so other grips and styles, too many to mention, which make you wonder what the professionals are trying to achieve. What it makes you understand though, is that professionals and amateurs alike struggle with their putting. And no matter how good or bad a golfer you are, the putting yips can hit anywhere, anytime. So, the first of the fundamentals you must consider is – putting style. If you want to get rid of all your putting troubles, you have to go back to basics and adopt the following.

Simply stated, it's as fool-proof as you can get.

It is a widely accepted fact that Ben Crenshaw is one of the greatest putters who ever played the game. You don't see Ben cramped up like a crab trying to slink out of its shell, or his hands gripping the shaft as if he doesn't know whether to putt the ball or drive the putter into the green. No, Ben is renowned for gripping the putter with a grip so light and gentle that the putter looks as if it could drop from his hands. The reason for that is simple. A gentle putting grip eliminates tension from the hands and arms, which is the first rule in improving your putting.

To work on adopting this putting style, the following exercises can be done in your own home, out of sight of other golfers, behind closed doors if you like, so you don't have to worry about making a fool of yourself – not that what you are about to try will do that anyway.

To begin, stand with your feet about shoulder-width apart, your arms hanging straight down from your shoulders, your eyes looking down on an imaginary ball. Make sure that your eyes are either directly over this ball, or a tad behind it. Do not set up with your eyes ahead of it. That will lead to more problems than it will solve. Trust me on that one.

Now hold the putter with a light grip – just like gentle Ben does – and without a ball, simply practice a pendulum swing back and through, back and through, back and through. Isn't it amazing how the putter doesn't drop from your grip? Now try that a dozen or so times until you begin to have a feel for it – back and through, as gently as you like. But make sure you eliminate head movement from your putting stroke. Your head must be perfectly still at all times, and the stroke should be nothing more than a gentle rocking of your shoulders, but most importantly, with no breaking of your wrists.

Let me repeat that. ***No breaking of your wrists***. None whatsoever. You must not break your wrists. No, not, never. Not even the tiniest of twinges. If you don't believe me, switch on the TV and tune into the Golf Channel and watch the pros putt. You need to understand that you never break your wrists during a putting stroke. Doing so simply injects a whole series of other problems into the mix, particularly in line and weight of the putt. So, read that phrase over and over, again and again, until you fully understand what it means. ***You do not break your wrists during a putt***. Your putting stroke is simply a pendulum, a rocking of your shoulders with your head perfectly still. So spend a few minutes right now rocking these shoulders, with the lightest grip you can achieve, letting your mind and your arms and hands become accustomed to what it feels like.

Once you feel you're ready, read on.

What I want you to do now, is to place a ball on the carpet about two feet from the wall, so that you'll putt the ball against the skirting board, or wall, so that it bounces back to you. This way, you don't have to disrupt your practice session while you chase after the ball to hit it again. This simple method is key to your success – the repetitive striking of the ball, using the same stroke again and again and again, with the ball returning each time, to be nudged onto the same spot, then stroked again, until you develop a sense of what a good putting stroke feels like – ***without breaking your wrists***.

This is the first step in learning how to putt like a pro.

CHAPTER 7

THE TRIGGER

That is all good and well, and you now know what a smooth putting stroke feels like. But what if you can't take the putter back without an overwhelming need to jerk, or twitch, or do a forward press before each stroke? – just like I used to suffer. It wouldn't matter how light your grip is, or how sweet the stroke is, if you can't start the putting stroke without twitching, then you're beaten from the word go. Right? Well, I'm happy to tell you that you're wrong, because I cured my putting by adopting the following.

The key to starting any smooth golf stroke, whether that be a drive, a fairway wood, a greenside chip, a bunker shot, a pitch, a putt, or any other kind of shot you want to make is – *you must have a **trigger***. Just watch how the pros prepare to hit a ball. They'll waggle their club, or shuffle their feet, or look at the hole a number of times, or adjust their posture, flex their legs, settle down, press back, or go through some other set routine before they pull the trigger and take the stroke.

It's the same in tennis. You've seen them, I'm sure. Every tennis pro has a pre-shot routine that they perform before they toss the ball for the serve – so many bounces of the ball, or tuck of the hair behind the ear, or spinning the racket in their grip, or a number of glances at the opponent. Each and every one of them has a set routine, a sequence of actions that they perform without fail, time and time again, before they make their play. That routine is their ***trigger***, the series of repetitive moves they all take, which ***allows their reflexes and muscle memory to take over on automatic*** and get the job done – where have you heard that before? How else can these professional golfers and tennis players execute perfect shots under the most extreme pressure when every single nerve ending in their body is screaming at them and firing all sorts of electrical signals to the brain? It is because they execute their strokes using ***muscle memory***.

Now before you throw your hands in the air and moan in despair that these pros have played the game for years, that they spend hours practising every single day, that not only are they unbelievably talented, but they have coaches, mentors, psychologists, whole teams of experts working exclusively with them on improving their game, and how in the world are you expected to be able to compare your game with theirs? – just settle down and relax, will you?

And read on.

CHAPTER 8

PRACTICE MAKES PERFECT

Some golfers, when they've just been beaten by an opponent, are happy to tell anyone who will listen to them, just how lucky their opponent was. Luck plays a part in golf – it's called the rub of the green – but there's more to playing golf well than relying on luck. I believe it was Gary Player who first said the more he practices the luckier he becomes. The message is clear to anyone who wants to listen – if you want to be good at anything in life, you must practice.

I can almost hear you complaining that you've got a pressurized job that keeps you busy over 60 hours every week. On top of that you've got family concerns that tie up so much of your spare time, that what I'm telling you is no use to you. It just doesn't work. How can you spend time on the course practicing for hour upon hour? Well, the answer is –

you can't, and you don't need to, and you're not going to.

Here's why.

How many putting strokes do you think you would have to make before your mind and your body began to develop a sense of muscle memory, so that you could make a perfect stroke every time without even thinking about it? I don't know, and neither do you, because we're all different. But for argument's sake, let's just say that you had to take one thousand putting strokes before you developed reasonable muscle memory. *One thousand*? That sounds like one hell of a lot of putts, doesn't it?

Well, let's look into that for a moment.

If you averaged thirty-six putts a round, that would equate to about twenty-eight rounds in order for you to make one thousand putts. And if you played one round of golf a day, it would take four full weeks – let's call it a month – to play twenty-eight rounds.

Of course, if all you want to do is practice your putting, you don't have to play a full round of golf at all, just go down to the practice green, and start putting. But no matter which way you look at it, one thousand putts is pretty intensive stuff.

What if I said that you could hit one thousand putts in less than an hour and a half? – one hour and twenty minutes, to be more exact in my case. Would that convince you that muscle memory for improving your putting is within your reach, no matter how busy you are at work? I bet you it does.

I'll explain to you shortly how it's done. But first, I want to tell you how to beat the putting freeze, the pre-stroke yips, how to take that putter head back with the smoothest of smooth strokes, without any jerks, without any forward presses or any other interfering motor control movements – by working on your own trigger.

Understanding and developing your own pre-shot routine – your trigger – is the absolute key to

allowing your reflexes and muscle memory to take over on automatic and get on with the job of stroking these putts.

Trust me on this. It really does work.

CHAPTER 9

STEP 2

DEVELOP YOUR PUTTING TRIGGER

What I am about to tell you might sound complicated. But it isn't. It's only the act of explaining it that perhaps comes across as being a tad complicated. If you can't take it in first time through, read it again, and again, and as many times as you feel you have to, so that you fully and completely understand the simplicity of it all.

Here goes.

Watch the pros when they're about to drive off the tee. They waggle the club, they look at the hole, they fiddle through all sorts of movements before they pull the trigger and launch that drive. But putting is different. You can't stand on the green waggling the putter before you make a putt – well, you can if you like, but not only would it look odd, you would miss more putts than you could possibly hole, which defeats the whole purpose. So how do you develop a trigger for putting when by definition you have to stand completely still? The answer is – by using your hands and your eyes.

Here's how it's done.

Go back to placing a golf ball two feet from the wall, then take your stance as if you are ready to putt. If the state of your putting is anything like mine once was, that would be as far as you could go before you had to do something else to trigger the putting stroke – in my case, that putt-destroying forward press. But the solution is to relax, as follows.

Grip that putter as gently as you can – just like when you first practiced that smooth putting stroke earlier – then let your fingers almost let go of the putter for just an instant. Don't worry about dropping the putter. You won't, because it's resting on the floor. Now re-grip it as gently as you can again, then almost let go of it once more. By repeating this gentle tightening and relaxing of your grip, you are preventing your hands and arms from creating any tension. Do that a dozen or so times, even more if you want to, just gently tightening and relaxing, tightening and relaxing, again and again and again, until you become familiar with that simple action – your putting grip as light as light can be – and confident that you can never accidentally drop the putter.

Now prepare for your trigger.

Focus your eyes on a spot on the skirting board, or bottom of the wall, just as if you're looking at the hole. Meanwhile, you're continuing to gently tighten and relax, tighten and relax, your grip. Now look down at the putter, as if you are about to make the putt. You're checking that the putter head is perpendicular to the line of your putt – that is, it's on the correct line. Now look back at that spot on the skirting board, still tightening and relaxing your grip as gently as you can.

Now you're ready for your trigger. Here it comes.

Return your eyes to the putter head at the same time as you gently tighten your grip. The very instant your focus on the putter head coincides with the tightening of your grip, take the putter back, then stroke through the ball – just like you practiced earlier with that smoother-than-smooth putting stroke in Chapter 6.

Don't worry if it sounds complicated and awkward. It's not. The trigger action is simplicity in motion. Basically, what you are trying to achieve is to perform the following three coincidental actions:

- The instant your eyes return from the hole and focus on the putter head
- at the same time as you gently tighten your grip and
- initiate the putting stroke.

The backward takeaway of the putter is almost like a continuation, if you like, of your eye movement from the hole to the putter head, although your eyes must never move beyond the ball. They must stop at the ball, and remain fully focused on it – and ultimately on the spot where the ball once was – as the putter head returns to stroke through the ball and send it rolling towards the hole.

If I try to describe it by referring only to your eyes, the trigger goes something like this – bearing in mind that with every change in focus of your eyes, your grip is gently relaxing and tightening, the hand and finger movement so slight that it's almost unnoticeable.

Begin with your focus on the putter head – you're aiming the putt – then shift your focus to the hole, then back to the putter head – you're making a final check on the direction of the putt – then to the hole again, then finally back to the putter head at the same time as you begin the putting stroke – your trigger.

You may find that your preference is to take one more look at the hole, maybe even a couple of more looks, before pulling the trigger. But I've found that the more looks you take, the more looks you feel you *need* to take, until your mind has you locked over the ball waiting to move. So I would urge you to get it correct right from the beginning, and train your mind and your body to take as few looks at the hole as possible.

By adopting and persevering with this technique you are performing a number of simple actions that done together make it impossible for you to yip any putt. Yes, you read that correctly, and I want you to read that again and again until you completely understand what this technique does for you – **it is *impossible* for you to yip any putt**.

And here's why.

You now have a solid putting stroke, a pendulum rocking of the shoulders, with your eyes above or just behind the ball, with absolutely no breaking of the wrists – none whatsoever. You now hold the putter with the most gentle of grips, which you tighten and relax before taking the putt, making it impossible for even the slightest tension to creep into your hands and arms. You now have a pre-shot routine, your trigger, which you will work on developing until it becomes second nature to you, thus ***allowing your reflexes and muscle memory to take over on automatic*** and get the job done.

Which brings me to the question I love to answer. How do you manage to make one thousand putts in under an hour and a half?

Here's how.

CHAPTER 10

STEP 3

DEVELOP YOUR PUTTING MUSCLE MEMORY

Go back to placing a golf ball no more than two feet from the wall, and take your putting stance. What I want you to do now, is to putt that ball against the wall, letting it bounce back to you each time, then nudging it back onto its spot for you to putt again. As you go through this repetitive action, all the while you will be tightening and relaxing your grip, focusing for an instant on a spot on the wall, then back to the putter head, and pulling the trigger.

It's important to understand that you are not going for accuracy here, nor are you spending time taking each putt. It doesn't matter if the ball bounces back at you at a slight angle, or rebounds too hard or too soft. It matters only that you continue to putt that ball against the wall again and again and again, understanding that each putting stroke is sending a message to your brain, logging it into the subconscious where it will be stored for later use. It's also important to understand that by doing this drill in this quick and repetitive manner, you are not allowing your mind to 'lock' onto the putt, and are ridding yourself of any subconscious need to take just one more look at the hole.

Now, I don't expect you to stand up against that wall for an hour and a half. Doing that would be enough for anyone to give up right there. No, I want you to take fifty putts only, and I want you to time yourself. It takes me roughly four minutes to take 50 two-foot putts, bouncing them off the wall like that, and I want you to aim for about that length of time, too. So once you've timed yourself, multiply that time by 20, and that will tell you how long it will take you to make one thousand putts. In other words, if you do that 50-putt routine twenty times, you will have made one thousand putts. But more importantly, you will have sent one thousand messages to your brain telling it how to perform a smooth, tension-free putt, and preparing it to ***allow your reflexes and muscle memory to take over on automatic*** and get the job done.

Once you've done your first fifty putts, I want you to take a break. Have a cup of coffee. Read a magazine. Watch the news. Check email. Do something, anything, to break the monotony of the routine. You can continue if you like, carry on for another fifty or more, but I've found that the 50-putt routine lets me fit it in anytime I like during my working day. And you can, too. I don't care how busy you claim to be. I don't care if you're working a hundred hours a week. If you can't find time in a 24-hour day to take a 4-minute break, then you can't find time to play golf at all – period – so the exercise is meaningless anyway.

Getting back to that first 50-putts, it's important not to worry if at first you still have a residual sense of your putting yips, that not all putts feel as smooth as you would like them to be, that it all feels kind of strange and awkward, and that you worry that it's not going to work. Do not worry. It will work. Trust me on that. I have absolutely no doubts at all, and neither will you after you have performed a number of 50-putt sessions.

It took me somewhere in the region of 500 putts before I had that first hint of a sense that I might finally be overcoming my putting yips, that I truly was onto something, that if I kept bouncing that ball off the skirting board, session after session, again and again, then I would be cured. Even 500 putts sounds a lot to take before I began to feel the debilitating effects of the yips leave my system. But 500 putts took me less than an hour. If I told you that you, too, could fix your putting in less than one hour, would you jump at it? You bet you would. You'd jump straight in with both feet.

And what I like most about this 50-putt technique is that it takes no time at all to complete – less than four minutes in my case – and that each 50-putt session can be done anytime you like, anywhere you like. First thing in the morning before you take a shower, then another 50 putts after your shower. Do a quick 50-putt session before breakfast, and another after, and you've completed 200 putts before you've even left home for the office. Do that every day, and you've done your thousand putts in one working week. Do you see how quickly you can rack up the number of putts? But importantly, every single putt you make is sending one more signal to your brain, setting it up to ***allow your reflexes and muscle memory to take over on automatic***.

You will also find that each 50-putt session becomes more and more enjoyable as you begin to feel more relaxed over the ball, as your putting stroke improves, and tension fades from your nervous system. And the more confident you become, the more you will want to carry on with these sessions. And why stop at one thousand? I didn't. If I'm being honest, it took me about another two thousand putts before I'd completely convinced myself that my putting yips really were gone for good. And even now, years later, I'll just pick up that putter and do another 50 putts – 4 minutes, that's all it takes.

So keep going. Go for two thousand, three thousand, even more. Believe me, if you once suffered from the yips and you begin to feel them evaporate, you'll want to putt another fifty balls just to prove to yourself that they really have gone. I would urge you to carry on with these 50-putt sessions for as long as you enjoy them – between breaks at work, at home, before you go to bed, when you get up in the morning, whenever, just slip in another 50 putts. It's fun, it's easy, and it's truly exhilarating when you realise your yips really are beginning to disappear. The 50-putt technique really does work.

But you're not done yet.

CHAPTER 11

STEP 4

DEVELOP YOUR PUTTING CONFIDENCE

Okay, you are now able to face that wall and make 50 putts against it time and time again with your tension-free stroke, and without even the slightest signs of any yips. Now comes the real test, taking everything you've practiced at home – the lightest of grips and your automatic trigger that sets off your smooth pendulum putting stroke – and trying it out for real on the golf course.

You can't wait. Of course you can't. But you also have a sense of trepidation, a worry, maybe even a deep-rooted fear that it won't work. That's perfectly natural. But it *will* work. Nothing's changed, except the putting surface. And, of course, the ball won't bounce back either. It'll disappear into the hole. Trust yourself. Believe in your ability. Your mind and body are now working together through self-taught muscle memory. But before you drive from that first tee, eager to get onto that green and start sinking putts, I want you to spend some time on the practice putting green, because I am about to introduce you to a putting drill that will improve your putting beyond your wildest dreams. And believe me when I say to you – ***this drill works***.

Here's how to do it.

It's all very well being able to putt tension-free with renewed confidence, but what many golfers don't do – without realising they're not doing it – is to putt out, that is to say, to actually putt the ball into the hole during a round of golf. Think about that. You're having an enjoyable round with your buddy, and you have a tricky ten footer which you putt with your new smooth putting stroke. The ball narrowly slides past the edge of the hole, maybe even lips out, and stops two feet away. Your buddy 'gives' you the return putt, and you thank him and pocket the ball. It would be rude, of course, to decline your buddy's kind gesture, and to putt out instead. But this is how the fear of these dreaded three-footers slowly and insidiously creeps back into the nervous system over time.

After playing a couple of rounds where you haven't been asked to hole a short putt for a while, all of a sudden the game's tight on the back nine and you're faced with a putt that's just beyond that 'friendly' range. Your buddy is unable to look you in the eye, because he wants you to putt out. As you walk towards the putt, doubt creeps in. You take your stance, you grit your teeth, you tighten your grip, and before you know it, you twitch at the putt and miss it. Suddenly, all the good work you've done, the repetitive drills, the tightening and relaxing of your grip, the pre-shot trigger routine, are all for nothing, and you feel as if you've landed back on square one.

But do not worry. Here's how to avoid that from happening – ***ever***.

What you have to do – ***and this is an absolute must*** if you want to keep your putting at its new improved level – is to ***practice holing out***. I can't impress enough upon you how critical this is. ***It is an absolute must that you practice holing out***. So before you rush onto that first tee – and you should do this before you begin any round – I want you to go to the practice putting green. Select a hole on a relatively flat part of the green – you're not going for difficulty here, just trying to train your mind into holing putts – then place four balls ***at different spots*** around that hole, no more than one foot from it. Take your time over each putt, remembering to tighten and relax your grip. Go through your pre-shot routine just like you've learned, pull the trigger, and one by one putt each ball into the hole. Now place the balls around the hole again, but this time no more than two feet away. Repeat the putting exercise, holing out each ball in turn. Now place the balls no more than three feet from the hole, and putt out again. Repeat again, each time placing the four balls one foot farther from the hole, and ***at different spots*** around the hole.

Sounds easy, doesn't it? In fact it's so easy it feels stupid and makes you not want to bother holing them out at all. They're all too short, aren't they? But regardless of how short these putts are, ***this is the most important drill you have to do if you want to overcome all your putting flaws***. By consistently holing out you are cementing in your brain your ability to sink putts from any short distance. Oh, I forgot to tell you, that if you miss one of these putts at any time from any distance, you have to stop right there and go back to the beginning, and place all four balls one foot from the hole again, and go through the whole process from the start.

Still think it's easy? Try it. See how far you get. If I were a betting man, I'd bet it'll take you a couple of weeks before you get beyond three feet, and you might never even manage that. And I would bet the farm that you never get beyond six feet – ***ever***. Remember that statistic that professional golfers hole only 50 per cent of six-foot putts? Now you understand how hard this is.

The strength of this drill is that it consolidates all you've learned in developing your new smooth putting stroke, as well as jacking up the pressure as you move the set of four balls farther and farther away from the hole. But importantly, it builds up muscle memory confidence, so that you no longer fear being asked to putt out from two or three feet, or to nail a tricky four-footer for the half. It also takes no time at all to do. You don't need to arrive for your scheduled round of golf a couple of hours early. All it takes is five minutes, ten tops, to give your brain a taste of holing out putts and, most importantly, stimulating that muscle memory.

And here's one golden tip to take away with you. When lining up your putt, rotate your ball so that the logo is aligned at your target. I use a slight variation to that, by rotating my ball so that the logo is parallel to my putter face. No matter which way you do it, this is a great tip to help you correctly align your putts all the time.

But one parting word of advice – please understand that you won't hole every putt you face. No one can. Not Tiger, not Jack, not even Ben, and certainly not you. There are too many variables in any putt – speed of the greens, break in the putt, spike-marks, specks of sand, and a whole bunch of other irregularities that you can't possibly account for. So be realistic in your expectations.

Now go out there and play golf without any fear on the greens. Why be afraid? You know how to hole these putts now. So start looking forward to absolutely nailing these nasty little four-footers to the back of the hole like a professional golfer. Trust your putting stroke. Don't even think about it. You've assigned it to muscle memory.

But remember – golf is only a game. Play it for exercise and fun. You won't hole every putt you come across, and you won't be expected to. But with your new improved putting stroke you're giving yourself every chance to do so. So go out there and play golf. Love the game. Relish the challenge. Believe in your putting stroke. And prove to yourself that you can putt as well as the best of them. I know you can.

In fact, show your buddies how you can now **PUTT LIKE A PRO**.

CHAPTER 12

ABOUT THE AUTHOR

Although Frank used to be a keen golfer, he is now more of an armchair sportsman than a participant, yet continues to proclaim his natural ability to birdie the 19th hole with astonishing regularity.

Born far too many years ago in Scotland, Frank graduated from Strathclyde University, Glasgow, with a degree he hated. He assures everyone who cares to listen, that he never really wanted to be a civil engineer, but with youthful apathy soon found himself working in Glasgow's Department of Architecture and Related Services designing sewerage schemes, and wondering how in the hell he got there, and what did he really want to do with his life. Working overseas sounded like a good idea, so off he went to the Middle East – Saudi Arabia, Qatar, Bahrain – then to the USA, where he worked and lived for over 20 years, regrettably as a civil engineer.

But working overseas helped Frank appreciate the raw beauty of his home country, and his love of reading fiction helped him understand that his true calling was to be a novelist. Now a dual US/UK citizen, Frank makes his home in the outskirts of Glasgow, where he writes his best-selling crime series set in – where else? – St. Andrews, the home of golf. Frank can often be seen carrying out some serious research in the old grey town's many pubs, all under the guise of practicing that 19th hole. Despite that, Frank assures his wife that he is working hard on his next crime novel.

Visit Frank's website at www.frankmuir.com for details of his crime novels. Frank writes under the author name T.F. Muir in the UK, and T. Frank Muir in the USA (for his first five books only), and complains that multiple author names are almost as confusing as civil engineering.

CHAPTER 13

OTHER BOOKS WRITTEN BY FRANK

Fiction:

Frank's best-selling DCI Gilchrist crime series set in St. Andrews, Scotland.

Author name – T.F. Muir

Eye for an Eye *

Hand for a Hand *

Tooth for a Tooth *

Life for a Life *

The Meating Room *

Blood Torment

The Killing Connection

Dead Catch

Dead Still

The Murder List

** Also published in the USA under the author name T. Frank Muir. All of Frank's books are now available in the USA, the most recent under the author name T.F. Muir – confusing, isn't it?*

Self-help:

Author name – Frank Muir

How to Chip Like a Pro – in 4 Simple Steps

How to Cure Your Putting Yips – in 4 Simple Steps

Joke Booklet:

Author name – Hopkins Muir

Shit Yourself Laughing – 20 of the best shit jokes

www.frankmuir.com

Printed in Dunstable, United Kingdom

73608570R00036